YOUR PASSPORT TO

TURKEY

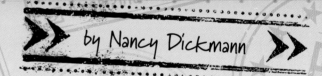

by Nancy Dickmann

CONTENT CONSULTANT

Nihal Caliskan, Turkish Language Lecturer,
SOAS University of London, UK

a capstone imprint

Capstone Captivate is published by Capstone Press, an imprint of Capstone.
1710 Roe Crest Drive
North Mankato, Minnesota 56003
www.capstonepub.com

Library of Congress Cataloging-in-Publication Data is available on the Library of Congress website.
ISBN: 978-1-4966-9555-0 (hardcover)
ISBN: 978-1-4966-9723-3 (paperback)
ISBN: 978-1-9771-5547-4 (eBook PDF)

33614082422527

Summary:
What would it be like to live in Turkey? How is Turkish culture unique? Explore the sights, traditions, and daily lives of people in Turkey.

Image Credits
Capstone: Eric Gohl, 5; Dreamstime: Laudibi, 8; Getty Images: OZAN KOSE/AFP, 25, Sedat Simsek/Anadolu Agency, 27; iStockphoto: benstevens, cover, lilagri, 19; Shutterstock: Everett Collection, 11, Gavran333, 23, Luciano Mortula - LGM, 20, muratart, 15, 17, Nejdet Duzen, 7, qvattro, 13, Smit, 14, Turkey Photo, 29

Design Elements
iStockphoto: Yevhenii Dubinko; Shutterstock: charnsitr, Filip Bjorkman, Flipser, MicroOne, pingebat

Editorial Credits
Editor: Clare Lewis; Designer: Juliette Peters;
Media Research: Tracy Cummins; Premedia: Laura Manthe

All internet sites appearing in back matter were available and accurate when this book was sent to press.

Printed and bound in the United States of America.   PO3837

CONTENTS

Words in **bold** are in the glossary.

CHAPTER ONE

WELCOME TO TURKEY!

Sparkling white stone terraces step down toward the valley floor. They look like a **petrified** waterfall. Each terrace is a shallow pool filled with pale blue water. The water is clear and warm. This is Pamukkale in Turkey. The ancient Greeks used to swim in these pools. Today, visitors come from all over the world to see them.

Turkey is a large country. It is unusual because it is part of two different **continents**. A small section in the northwest is part of Europe. The rest of the country is in Asia. Narrow channels of water separate the two parts. This location has made Turkey an important region since ancient times.

MAP OF TURKEY

Istanbul
Blue Mosque
Topkapi Palace
Hagia Sophia

Ani

ANKARA

Mount Ararat

TURKEY

Lake Van

Troy

Izmir

Göreme

Ephesus
Pamukkale

Antalya

Burning
Rock

N
W   E
S

- ■ Capital City
- ● City
- ⬡ Landform
- ▲ Landmarks

Explore Turkey's cities
and landmarks.

FACT FILE

GEOGRAPHY: Turkey's European part has borders with Greece, Bulgaria, and Azerbaijan. The Asian section borders Georgia, Armenia, Iran, Iraq, and Syria. There are also many small islands.

NATURAL RESOURCES: Turkey has oil, gas, and coal, and metals such as iron, copper, and gold. It also grows tobacco, cotton, and olives.

EAST MEETS WEST

The Asian part of Turkey is called Anatolia. It is sometimes called Asia Minor. The European part is called Thrace. Turkey's culture is a mix of east and west. Most people are Muslim. Many parts have a Middle Eastern feel. But it also looks more European than other countries in the region.

In ancient times, many trading ships stopped in Izmir. Back then it was called Smyrna.

LAND AND SEA

Turkey has a long coastline. The Mediterranean Sea lies to the south and west. The Black Sea is to the north. Several countries, including Russia, border the Black Sea. The only way from there to the Mediterranean is through Turkey. In ancient times, Turkey was an important stop on many trade routes.

CHAPTER TWO

HISTORY OF TURKEY

Turkey is home to some of the world's oldest civilizations. One of the world's first cities was founded there. It was built nearly 9,000 years ago. Other cities were soon built across Turkey.

Archaeologists have found cave paintings in ancient Turkish cities.

ONE LAND, MANY RULERS

Many different groups have controlled Turkey. The Hittites were very powerful. They often fought against the Egyptians. Later, the Greeks ruled parts of Turkey. So did the Persians. There were many battles. In the 300s BCE Alexander the Great pushed the Persians out. At one point, the Romans took over.

In 285 BCE the Roman **Empire** split in two. The eastern half included Turkey. Its capital was Constantinople. This city is now called Istanbul. The Turks reached the area around 1000 CE. They came from central Asia.

TROY

The ancient Greeks had many legends. One was about a war that lasted ten years. The Greeks were trying to conquer the city of Troy. They finally succeeded by hiding soldiers inside a hollow wooden horse. The legend may not be true, but Troy was a real place. In the 1800s, archaeologists discovered its remains in northwest Turkey.

TIMELINE OF TURKISH HISTORY

ABOUT 6700 BCE: Çatalhöyük, one of the world's first cities, is built.

ABOUT 1650–1180 BCE: The Hittites rule Anatolia.

546 BCE: The Achaemenid Empire, based in Persia, takes over Anatolia.

334 BCE: Alexander the Great forces the Persians out.

330 CE: Constantinople becomes the capital of the eastern Roman Empire.

ABOUT 1000: The Turks arrive in Anatolia from central Asia.

ABOUT 1300: The Ottoman Empire begins.

1453: The Ottomans conquer Constantinople and make it their capital.

1914–1918: The Ottoman Empire fights in World War I.

1922: The Ottoman Empire comes to an end.

1923: Turkey is officially declared to be a republic.

THE OTTOMAN EMPIRE

The Turks took over more land. By the 1500s, they controlled a large area. It was called the Ottoman Empire. It lasted until World War I. The Ottomans fought on the side of Germany. But they lost. After the war, the empire was broken up.

Mustafa Kemal was an army officer. He didn't want other countries to **occupy** Turkey. He forced them out. Then he set up a new **parliament**. This was the **Republic** of Turkey. Kemal took the name "Atatürk." It means "Father of the Turks."

MODERN TURKEY

Atatürk wanted Turkey to be more modern. He encouraged Turks to leave some traditional ways of life behind. He changed the government of Turkey. It became less based on religion and more on democracy.

Atatürk served as president of Turkey until his death in 1938.

CHAPTER THREE

EXPLORE TURKEY

Turkey is a land of great natural beauty. Much of the country is covered in mountains. The tallest is Mount Agri, also known as Mount Ararat, in the east. It is 16,945 feet (5,165 meters) tall. Another mountain slope is the site of the "Burning Rock." Flickering flames burn day and night. They are fed by natural gas seeping from the rocks.

FACT

The burning rock is also known as the Chimaera. This name comes from a fire-breathing monster from Greek mythology.

BEACHES AND LAKES

Turkey has a long coastline, with many islands. It also has a warm climate. Tourists come to visit its beautiful beaches. Many of the best beaches are in the southwest. Mountains reach down to the sea. The water is a beautiful shade of blue.

More than 50 million people visit Turkey each year. Many of them come for the sun and sand.

People also visit Lake Van. This deep lake is surrounded by mountains. Birdwatchers can spot pelicans and flamingos in its waters.

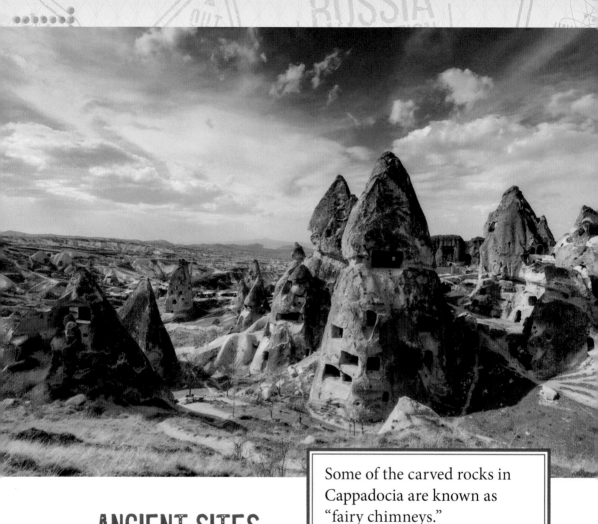

Some of the carved rocks in Cappadocia are known as "fairy chimneys."

ANCIENT SITES

Turkey's long history means that there are many ancient sites. The region of Cappadocia is in the center. It has stunning rock formations. There are also many caves. People have lived in them for thousands of years. In some places, buildings are cut into the soft volcanic rock. Near the town of Göreme, there are beautiful rock-cut churches.

Long ago, this building in Ephesus was one of the largest libraries in the world.

The Greeks and Romans also left their mark on Turkey. The city of Ephesus is in western Turkey. Many buildings from this time period still stand. There are **temples**, houses, and a large theater.

SILK ROAD

The Silk Road was an ancient route linking China to Europe. It passed through Turkey. Caravans of traders traveled through the region. Many of them stopped in the city of Ani. It is now an eerie ghost town. Crumbling buildings provide a window into the past.

ISTANBUL

Istanbul is one of the world's most beautiful cities. It is also one of the most exciting. Half of it is in Europe. The other half is in Asia. Istanbul has been the capital of several empires. It is not Turkey's capital, but it is the largest city.

Tourists come to see Istanbul's historic buildings. These include the Blue **Mosque** and Topkapi Palace. There are also busy markets and shops. There are many cafés and food stalls.

HAGIA SOPHIA

The Hagia Sophia is an enormous cathedral in Istanbul. Its name means "holy wisdom." It was completed in 537 CE. Its huge dome is a marvel of engineering. It was originally a Christian church. But when the Muslim Ottomans took over, they turned it into a mosque. Atatürk made it into a museum in 1934. But in 2020, Turkey's president declared that it would once more be a mosque.

Antalya was once a Roman port. Its beaches and harbor attract many tourists.

ANKARA

Atatürk chose the small town of Ankara as Turkey's capital. It is now a bustling modern city. Outside the old town, there are many 21st-century buildings. It is less crowded than Istanbul. There are more green spaces.

CHAPTER FOUR

DAILY LIFE

Around three-quarters of people in Turkey live in cities. There are factories, offices, and suburbs, like in any European city. Most people wear western-style clothes. Turkish cities also have markets, with stalls lined up side-by-side. Some markets sell food. Others have stalls selling clothing, tools, jewelry, and more.

Life in the countryside is different. Several generations often live together. Many people work on farms. They grow grains and vegetables. They also grow hazelnuts, figs, and apricots. People in villages are more likely to wear traditional clothing. This includes baggy trousers for men and women.

FACT

Most people in Turkey speak Turkish. This language was once written using Arabic script. In 1928, Atatürk decided it should be written in the Latin alphabet instead.

In some parts of Turkey, people live in tents, herding goats or sheep from place to place.

The Blue Mosque is one of Istanbul's top sights. The inside is decorated with blue tiles.

RELIGION IN TURKEY

More than 95 percent of people in Turkey are Muslim. But religion and government are kept separate. This was Atatürk's vision for Turkey. It is called **secularism**. Religion is still important to many people. Islam is taught in schools. Some women wear headscarves.

Muslims worship in mosques. Turkey has more than 80,000 of them! Some are small and simple. Others are huge and richly decorated. Some mosques are very old. The call to prayer rings out five times a day. In the past, a person called out from a tower. Now, loudspeakers are often used instead.

THE KURDS

About one-fifth of Turkey's population belong to a group called the Kurds. Kurds are Muslim too. But they have their own culture and language. The Kurds mainly live in southeast Turkey. There are also many Kurds in neighboring Iraq and Iran. Some people want all Kurds to join together to form their own country. This has sometimes led to fighting in Turkey.

FOOD AND DRINK

Turkey is known for its delicious food. Turkish food is usually not very spicy. At some restaurants, the food is served on a low table. People sit on cushions on the floor. Meals often start with a selection of small dishes. These are called meze.

MEAT DISHES

Kebap is one of the most famous dishes. There are many different versions. Sometimes the meat is on skewers. It can be served in pita bread. One type has strips of lamb cooked in tomato sauce.

Turks also love meatballs called köfte. They can be eaten plain or in a sandwich. They are sometimes put into a stew. Little dumplings called manti are also popular. They are filled with meat, like mini ravioli. Manti usually comes with tomato sauce. Yogurt is also served with many dishes, including köfte.

Baklava is a sweet treat made from pastry, nuts, and syrup.

MENEMEN

Menemen is a popular breakfast dish. Some people like to add spinach, sausage, or cheese. You will need an adult to help you.

Ingredients:
- olive oil
- onion
- green pepper
- can of chopped tomatoes
- 4 eggs
- 1 tablespoon butter
- salt and pepper

Instructions:

1. Chop the onion and pepper.
2. Heat some olive oil in a pan and sauté the vegetables until they are soft.
3. Stir in the chopped tomatoes and butter, and season with salt and pepper.
4. Once the tomatoes are hot, crack the eggs directly into the pan. Let them cook for a moment, then stir them into the mixture.
5. Keep cooking until the eggs are cooked the way you like. Serve with fresh bread.

23

CHAPTER FIVE

HOLIDAYS AND CELEBRATIONS

Some celebrations in Turkey are religious. Ramadan is an important festival for Muslims. In Turkey, it is called Ramazan. For a month, people fast. They do not eat from sunrise to sunset. After sunset, they share a meal with family. At the end of Ramazan there is a big celebration. Children watch shadow puppet shows. People give gifts and eat sweets.

FACT

Muslims in Turkey also celebrate Eid al-Adha. It lasts for four days. People sometimes **sacrifice** an animal to share with family and neighbors. They also give some meat to the poor.

At Nowruz, some people jump over the bonfires!

NEW YEAR

Turks celebrate a festival called Nowruz in March. It is the Persian new year. People gather together to welcome the spring. They share food and recite poetry. Many people wear colorful clothes and wave flags. They build bonfires on mountains. Then they dance around the bonfires.

NATIONAL HOLIDAYS

Atatürk believed children were the future of Turkey. He dedicated April 23 to them. Schools close for the day. Children can sit in Parliament. On May 19 young people honor Atatürk by playing sports. There are parades with flags.

August 30 is Victory Day. It celebrates the end of the war for Turkey's **independence**. There are ceremonies and flying displays. People hang flags. They display pictures of Atatürk. On October 29, people remember the time that Turkey became a republic.

THE MESIR PASTE FESTIVAL

Some celebrations in Turkey are much more unusual. One is based on a legend from Ottoman times. It told of the invention of a new medicine. Today, people make the healing paste and wrap it in paper. Then it is blessed and scattered from the roof of a mosque. If you catch a piece, you will have good luck.

People believe that eating the sweet paste will improve health.

CHAPTER SIX

SPORTS AND RECREATION

Soccer is Turkey's most popular sport. The country played in the World Cup for the first time in 1954. The top teams play in European competitions. Two of them are based in Istanbul. Galatasaray are from the European part of the city. Fenerbahçe play in the Asian half. The clubs have a fierce rivalry.

WRESTLING

Oil wrestling is Turkey's national sport. Its history goes back centuries. Wrestlers cover their bodies in oil. Then they try to pin their opponent down. The oil makes them slippery and hard to hold. Skill is more important than strength. People compete in modern forms of wrestling too. Most of Turkey's Olympic medals are for wrestling.

One oil wrestling competition has been held annually since the 1300s.

CEVIZ OYUNU

This popular children's game is easy to play. Its name means "walnut game." It can be played by two or more people.

1. Pound a nail into the ground and balance a coin on top.
2. Each player starts with an equal number of walnuts. They take turns throwing a walnut at the coin.
3. If you knock the coin off the nail, put it back in place and wait nearby. When the other players miss the coin, you get to pick up their walnuts.
4. If another player knocks the coin off, they take your place collecting walnuts.
5. The game ends when one player has all the walnuts.

GLOSSARY

archaeologist (are-kee-OL-uh-jist)
a person who studies human history by digging historic sites and finding things

continent (KON-ti-nunt)
one of the seven large masses that Earth's land is divided into

empire (EM-pire)
a large area of land ruled over by a single person or group

independence (in-de-PEN-duhns)
the state of not being ruled over by anyone else

mosque (MOSK)
a building where Muslims gather to pray

occupy (OCK-yoo-pie)
to take control of a country and station soldiers there

parliament (PAR-luh-ment)
a body made up of elected representatives who make laws

petrified (PET-ri-fide)
turned into stone

republic (ri-PUB-lick)
a state that is run by elected officials rather than by a king or queen

sacrifice (SACK-ruh-fyse)
to kill an animal or give up a possession as an offering to a god

secularism (SEK-yuh-luh-riz-uhm)
the idea that religion and government should be kept separate

temple (TEM-puhl)
a sacred building where religious rituals take place

READ MORE

Cline, Bev. *Turkey*. Calgary, Alberta: Lightbox, 2018.

DeCarlo, Carolyn. *The Ottoman Empire*. New York: Rosen Education Service, 2018.

Robinson, Joanna J. *Turkey*. North Mankato, MN: The Child's World, 2015.

INTERNET SITES

Encyclopedia Britannica: Fast Facts About Turkey
britannica.com/place/Turkey

National Geographic Kids: Turkey Facts
kids.nationalgeographic.com/explore/countries/turkey/

Science Kids: Turkey Facts
sciencekids.co.nz/sciencefacts/countries/turkey.html

INDEX

OTHER BOOKS IN THIS SERIES

YOUR PASSPORT TO ARGENTINA

YOUR PASSPORT TO CHINA

YOUR PASSPORT TO ECUADOR

YOUR PASSPORT TO EL SALVADOR

YOUR PASSPORT TO ETHIOPIA

YOUR PASSPORT TO FRANCE

YOUR PASSPORT TO GUATEMALA

YOUR PASSPORT TO IRAN

YOUR PASSPORT TO ITALY

YOUR PASSPORT TO KENYA

YOUR PASSPORT TO PERU

YOUR PASSPORT TO RUSSIA

YOUR PASSPORT TO SOUTH KOREA

YOUR PASSPORT TO SPAIN

YOUR PASSPORT TO SRI LANKA

YOUR PASSPORT TO TURKEY